The Partition of British India: The History and Le[gacy of the] British Raj into India and Pak[istan]

By Charles River Editors

The British Raj's flag

About Charles River Editors

Charles River Editors is a boutique digital publishing company, specializing in bringing history back to life with educational and engaging books on a wide range of topics. Keep up to date with our new and free offerings with this 5 second sign up on our weekly mailing list, and visit Our Kindle Author Page to see other recently published Kindle titles.

We make these books for you and always want to know our readers' opinions, so we encourage you to leave reviews and look forward to publishing new and exciting titles each week.

Introduction

A depiction of the Queen's Own Madras Sappers and Miners, 1896

The British Raj

"A significant fact which stands out is that those parts of India which have been longest under British rule are the poorest today. Indeed some kind of chart might be drawn up to indicate the close connection between length of British rule and progressive growth of poverty." - Jawaharlal Nehru, *The Discovery of India*

The British East India Company served as one of the key players in the formation of the British Empire. From its origins as a trading company struggling to keep up with its superior Dutch, Portuguese, and Spanish competitors to its tenure as the ruling authority of the Indian subcontinent to its eventual hubristic downfall, the East India Company serves as a lens through which to explore the much larger economic and social forces that shaped the formation of a global British Empire. As a private company that became a non-state global power in its own right, the East India Company also serves as a cautionary tale all too relevant to the modern world's current political and economic situation.

On its most basic level, the East India Company played an essential part in the development of long-distance trade between Britain and Asia. The trade in textiles, ceramics, tea, and other goods brought a huge influx of capital into the British economy. This not only fueled the Industrial Revolution, but also created a demand for luxury items amongst the middle classes.

The economic growth provided by the East India Company was one factor in Britain's ascendancy from a middling regional power to the most powerful nation on the planet. The profits generated by the East India Company also created incentive for other European powers to follow its lead, which led to three centuries of competition for colonies around the world. This process went well beyond Asia to affect most of the planet, including Africa and the Middle East.

Beyond its obvious influence in areas like trade and commerce, the East India Company also served as a point of cultural contact between Western Europeans, South Asians, and East Asians. Quintessentially British practices such as tea drinking were made possible by East India Company trade. The products and cultural practices traveling back and forth on East India Company ships from one continent to another also reconfigured the way societies around the globe viewed sexuality, gender, class, and labor. On a much darker level, the East India Company fueled white supremacy and European concepts of Orientalism.

Ultimately, the company's activity across the Indian subcontinent led to further British involvement there, and the British Raj, a period of British dominance and rule over India that formally began in 1857 and lasted until 1947, remains a highly debated topic amongst historians, political scientists, the British people, and the people of modern India. In Martin Deming Lewis's *British in India: Imperialism or Trusteeship*, he attempts to settle the question, opening with opposing views of those closest to British India:

> "No romance can compare with the story of the handful of Englishmen . . . who, beginning as mere traders and merchant settlers, have in barely two centuries built up the majestic structure of an Imperial system under which peace, order and good government are secured for three hundred and fifty millions of human beings inhabiting what is in essence a continent of its own." - A 1942 Raj official

> "Those parts of India which have been longest under British rule are the poorest today. . . Nearly all our major problems today have grown up during British rule and as a direct result of British policy: the princes; the minority problem; various vested interests, foreign and Indian; the lack of industry and the neglect of agriculture; the extreme backwardness in the social services; and, above all, the tragic poverty of the people." - Jawaharal Nehru, imprisoned Indian reformer, 1944

How can it be that two contemporaries view the same phenomenon so differently? Without a full understanding of the Raj, simplifications and hastily-drawn conclusions are the only possible outcomes. Instead, it's necessary to seek an understanding of the people, forces, and events shaping the history of British India to arrive at valid conclusions about the British-Indian experience and to understand the continued divide over its legacy. Perhaps then it's possible to answer Lewis's question: "Is it possible that British rule was both destructive and creative at the same time?"[1]

Thanks to its commercial complexion and the power invested in a board of directors, British rule in India was characterized by economic monopolies, aggressive trade practices, punitive taxation, and the impoverishment of vast regions of India. Much of the Company's industry was based on a policy of producing and exporting raw materials from India and importing manufactured goods to satisfy an almost unlimited local market. Home industries and the domestic cottage textile industry, in particular, were heavily impacted by this, and with the addition of land taxes and a general regime of economic exploitation, the British East India Company grew to be a heavy burden on the shoulders of ordinary Indians.

After the Sepoy Rebellion, India was governed directly from Whitehall through a dedicated department: the India Office, headed by the Secretary of State for India. The territory was divided into 'British India', which came under direct British control, and the Princely States. The latter were the territories and sovereignties of various powerful tradition leaders, remnants of the old system of rule, who were permitted, under various weights of British superintendentship, to maintain their positions and continue their rule.

British India ultimately covered some 54 percent of the landmass and 77 percent of the population. By the time the British began to contemplate a withdrawal from India, 565 princely states were officially recognized, in addition to thousands of zamindaris and jagirs, which were in effect feudal estates. The stature of each Princely State was defined by the number of guns fired in salute upon a ceremonial occasion honoring one or other of the princes. These ranged from nine-gun to twenty-one-gun salutes and, in a great many cases, no salute at all.

The Princely States were reasonably evenly spread between ancient Muslim and Hindu dynasties, but bearing in mind the minority status of Muslims in India, Muslims were disproportionately represented. This tended to grant Muslims an equally disproportionate share of what power was devolved to local leaderships, and it positioned powerful Muslim leaders to exert a similarly unequal influence on British policy.

It stands to reason, therefore, as India began the countdown to independence after World War II, that the Indian Muslim leadership would begin to express anxiety over the prospect of universal suffrage and majority rule. At less than 20 percent of the population, Indian Muslims would inevitably find themselves overwhelmed by the Hindu majority, and as the British prepared to divest themselves of India, ancient enmities between Hindu and Muslim, long papered over by the secular and remote government of Britain, began once again to surface.

The Partition of British India: The History and Legacy of the Division of the British Raj into India and Pakistan looks at the complicated process by which the British partitioned British India. Along with pictures and a bibliography, you will learn about the partition like never before.

---

[1] Martin Deming Lewis, ed., British in India: Imperialism or Trusteeship? (Boston: D.C. Heath, 1962), vii.

The Partition of British India: The History and Legacy of the Division of the British Raj into India and Pakistan

About Charles River Editors

Introduction

   The Sepoy Rebellion and the End of the East India Company

   The Raj

   The Hindu-Muslim Divide

   Planning the Partition

   Violence

   Online Resources

   Bibliography

Free Books by Charles River Editors

Discounted Books by Charles River Editors

The Sepoy Rebellion and the End of the East India Company

British governance in India before the Raj is not easily explained. Regional differences and changing circumstances make simple description difficult, but a good general rule of the period is to understand that the East India Company was given major leeway to govern by the British crown. But all along, as the ultimate authority over English businesses interests and citizens overseas, the British government was within its rights to rule far more directly; it was merely content to allow the Company to work out its own governing policies, sharing power with local and regional Indian authorities.

In Bengal, the region where the rebellion that would change British-Indian relations permanently took place, the Company shared power with a local nawab. The Company was given increasing responsibility, including the power to collect taxes, or Diwani,[2] in 1773. Many have criticized this "Dual Authority" of both local Indian rulers and the rule of Company officials as allowing for greater corruption and creating anger and resentment throughout Bengal.[3] Though a defender of Britain's contributions to India's history and economy, Kartar Lalvani calls the Company's collection of the Diwani "short-sighted greed" and charges the Company with a "horrendous blunder concerning the role of revenue collection."[4]

To the Indian people, the events of 1857 are known as the first War for Independence. For the British, the time is referred to as a mutiny, an uprising, or a rebellion.[5] It is ironic that a similar story played out just under 100 years earlier, during the American Revolution, or as the Americans called it, the War for Independence.

Whatever the moniker, in 1857, one of the Indian armies, the Bengal, mutinied.[6] In the most cursory histories of the period, the cause of the rebellion is simply cited as an oversight, a change in the type of grease used in powder cartridges rumored to contain animal fat. This revelation horrified both Hindus and Muslims. The British response, which either failed to recognize the need to address the growing rumors or attempted to force Muslim and Hindu soldiers to use the ammunition despite their objections, made things worse. Author John McLeod explains that though the controversy over animal-greased rifle cartridges was the immediate cause of the conflict, economic, religious, and political resentment existed and had been worsening throughout 1856.[7] He also argues that rather than the uprising being attributable to either one incident or one cause - such as concerns over attempts at religious conversion by Christian officers, anger at the British in general, or frustration over specific tax policies - the rebellion was fueled not only by those with specific complaints against the British, but by those who

---

[2] Percival Griffiths, The British Impact on India (London: MacDonald, 1952), 77.
[3] Ibid., 143-7.
[4] Ibid., 10.
[5] John Keay, India: A History. New York: Atlantic Monthly Press, 2000. 437.
[6] John McLeod, The History of India (Westport, CT: Greenwood Press, 2002), 81.
[7] Ibid.

sought to end up on the right sight of history. McLeod argues that many Indians joined the rebellion only after the tide seemed to be turning in favor of Indian rebels: "In general, the deciding factor was whether or not such leaders felt that their interests and those of the people under their command would be best served by ending British rule."[8] McLeod concludes that the basis of the mutiny was ultimately economic, observing that "the commercial and educated classes of Calcutta, Bombay, and Madras had prospered under Company dominance, and held back."[9]

The rebellion was filled with internal conflict and rivalries among various groups, but one would be hard-pressed to find an author who does not cite the uprising of the Bengals as a turning point in British-Indian relations.[10] Though the cartridges greased with animal fat were withdrawn from service almost as quickly as they had appeared, the damage had already been done. The newly issued rifles required these cartridges to be opened with teeth prior to being jammed in the barrel of the rifle.[11] Long-term resentment toward British expectations and demands boiled over since "to cow-reverencing Hindus as to pig-paranoid Muslims the new ammunition could not have been more disgusting had it been smeared with excrement; nor, had it been dipped in hemlock, could it have been more deadly to their religious prospects."[12] Rumors about the British "tricks" spread quickly, as did resentment and mistrust.

An estimated 80,000 Indians and over 5,000 British were killed during the rebellion, often horrifically. As British historian Percival Griffiths said of the rebellion in retrospect, "It is useless to pass judgment on these excesses on both sides. Cruelty begets cruelty, and after a certain stage of suffering and horror justice and judgment give way to the demand for vengeance. All that can be said is that both amongst Indians and English the Mutiny brought out the best and the worst."[13]

Once it had put a stop to the rebellion by defeating the various Indian rebel groups individually,[14] the British government end up ruling India directly. However, as McLeod pointed out, "Like much of British imperial expansion, taking formal control of India was not intentional. Instead when British lives and trading interests (represented by the East India Company) were threatened by violent reaction to encroaching westernization, London felt obligated to step in to take control of both the situation and the country."[15] The news was delivered to the Indian people in a proclamation by the English government in 1858.[16]

---

[8] John McLeod, The History of India (Westport, CT: Greenwood Press, 2002), 82.
[9] Ibid.
[10] John Keay, 437.
[11] Ibid., 438.
[12] Ibid.

[14] John McLeod, 83.
[15] Robert Carr, "Concession & Repression: British Rule in India 1857-1919: Robert Carr Assesses the Nature of British Rule in India during a Key, Transitional Phase," *History Review*, no. 52 (2005).

At the highest levels, the new administrative structure of India was out of the new India Office and headed, at home, by the Secretary of State for India. In India, a new title–viceroy–was added to the position of governor-general, signifying that the authority now held the weight of the crown.[17]

Why did the British desire to continue their reign in India despite the bloody rebellion of 1857? McLeod cautions against a too ready acceptance of any single purpose. Rather than seeing India as a purely economic venture or only a source of international empire, the British desired to keep India within the empire for multiple and changing reasons. Certainly, there were economic benefits for Britain, as 25% of Indian taxes ended up in the mother country for administrative purposes, retirement pensions for former Indian officers, and as interest on loans made to India.[18] Acknowledging the economic factors, however, should not allow for the discounting of others, including Britain's desire to maintain her holdings in the East; to influence India religiously, educationally, and culturally; and to maintain her own image as a dominant power.[19]

Though the proposal was raised far earlier in 1858, it was not until 1877 that Queen Victoria was named the "Empress of India," in a ceremony held in Delhi.[20] The interest in expansion of nations like Russia, Austria, and a relatively new German nation-state eager to make a reputation, led Victoria to believe the title of empress would raise her status from "petulant widow to imperial matriarch."[21] These "psychological" concerns must weigh as heavily as the economic ones in understanding the desire for continued British dominance of India.

---

[16] Sneh Mahajan, British Foreign Policy, 1874-1914: The Role of India (London: Routledge, 2002), 37.
[17] McLeod, 83.
[18] Ibid., 84.
[19] Ibid.
[20] Sneh Mahajan.
[21] Ibid.

Queen Victoria

A formal portrait of Victoria as Empress of India

An Indian coin depicting the queen

Though it had been decided that the rule of India would continue under the Raj, the way in which the relationship between Britain and India would be viewed had yet to be determined. For many British thinkers, the mutiny "left a lasting mark on both the style and the ideology of British rule."[22] Though the liberals believed India could be westernized and modernized through a combination of education and political cooperation, based on "the gratitude and appreciation of the ruled…These beliefs had proved to be illusions."[23] Instead, the bloody mutiny confirmed in the minds of many Brits that India was and would remain a group destined for Western subjugation, ruled, albeit benevolently, by racial superiors. Albertini and Wirz explain, "This was henceforth the ideological basis of the British Raj. Although the other things the English brought India–domestic peace, a unified legal system, and modern administration–were also considered to legitimize British rule, the implicit or stated conviction remained, that India now "belonged" to England and that Indians were incompetent to rule themselves or manage their own affairs; as indeed were all nonwhite races."[24]

The India Office understood the need to avoid another rebellion, and they also knew that to rule British India effectively, it must have the support of nearly the whole land. Thus, the British increased the presence of British officers in India, but also concentrated on making alliances with Indian rulers in non-British regions of India, who were guaranteed their lands would never be annexed by the Crown in return for their loyalty. In its 1858 Royal Message, it was declared "that the British 'desire no extension of [our] present territorial possession and would respect the rights, dignity and honour of the native princes as our own.' States and territories, large and

---

[22] Rudolf Von Albertini and Albert Wirz, European Colonial Rule, 1880-1940: The Impact of the West on India, Southeast Asia, and Africa, trans. John G. Williamson (Westport, CT: Greenwood Press, 1982), 7.
[23] Ibid., 8.
[24] Ibid.

small, that had come under British rule during the expansionist phase as a result of protectorate and subsidiary treaties, retained the same status."[25] Those who had remained faithful to Britain during the rebellion were highly rewarded.[26]

To aid in the rule of the Indian people, the British established a new Indian Civil Service with a dedication to maintaining and promoting fair policy and rooting out corrupt practices.[27] The Civil Service employed British officers, but also many Indian civil servants who worked in India's provinces. The officers were described by one British-Indian writer as "minutely just, scrupulously honest, and inflexibly upright, introducing the culture and tradition of impartial and good governance without corruption."[28] The Indian Civil Service, which commentator after commentator mentions as an astounding example of fair and peaceful rule of many by the few, soon became known as "the steel frame" of India.[29]

The Raj

A depiction of Viceroy Lord Canning meeting Maharaja Ranbir Singh of Jammu &

---

[25] Rudolf Von Albertini and Albert Wirz, European Colonial Rule, 1880-1940: The Impact of the West on India, Southeast Asia, and Africa, trans. John G. Williamson (Westport, CT: Greenwood Press, 1982), 12.
[26] McLeod, 85.
[27] Kartar Lalvani, *The Making of India: The Untold Story of British Enterprise.* (London: Bloomsbury Continuum, 2016), 13.
[28] Ibid., 14.
[29] Ibid.

Kashmir in March 1860

The office of Secretary of State for India was a new one for Britain. The secretary's office was located in London, and the name of his department, the India Office.[30] The Sepoy Rebellion of 1857 had illustrated the horrors of widespread mutiny. As the British crown took over administration of the country, ratios were placed on the British Army which prevented the number of Indian soldiers to British from exceeding 3 to 1.[31] This proved difficult to enforce, as the expense of stationing and maintaining British troops overseas in these ratios was expensive.

[30] Percival Griffiths., 83.
[31] Pradeep P. Barua, Gentlemen of the Raj: The Indian Army Officer Corps, 1817-1949 (Westport, CT: Praeger, 2003), 3.

The first Secretary of State for India in 1874, Robert Arthur Talbot Gascoyne-Cecil

The debate over the long-term effects on the Raj continues today. Colonial India, it is said by critics, was little more than a storehouse of raw materials and a market for British goods and her world empire. Others argue that though there were long- and short-term problems with the Raj, the British should receive credit for some contributions to India's benefit. These include the establishment of law and order that led to greater domestic peace and the extensive civil administration system that allowed the country of 347 million to function. In its 1958 report on "The New India," the Planning Commission of the Indian government celebrated India's new found independence, but stopped short of critiquing their former colonial masters, claiming, "The British withdrew from India in a manner honorable to both sides and worthy of their own rich tradition of freedom, leaving a fund of goodwill and eagerness on the part of India to forgive and forget and to remember only the best of the past."[32] The "best," according to government officials, included a "strong administrative structure of the former Government," a highly trained and organized" Indian Civil Service, and "the judiciary and police system which had established both a mechanism and respect for law and order over the entire country."[33]

To rule such a massive country as India required an efficient administration and many bureaucrats to carry out the everyday work of governing. The Indian Civil Service, in its earliest form established in 1757, did just that. At first, the Indian Civil Service was dominated by Britons with only a few, narrowly selected Indians who had attended university in England and passed the Civil Service exams in London. Eventually, the Indian Civil Service became a home for aspiring classes of Indian professionals, who, after 1923, could take the Civil Service exam (though still in English) without leaving the country.[34] After passing the exam, however, ICS recruits spent time in Britain, taking classes and acquiring the "British social graces" necessary for service to the Crown.[35]

Members of the ICS had a remarkable amount of independence, charged with administering their assigned colonial areas with little interference or direct supervision after an initial period of training under a British officer. At only 25 or 30, a member of the service would carry out British policy, largely improvising their own responses to crisis or challenge, since communication was rare and difficult.[36] These young men, however, also carried out their role in a way that restored confidence in the fairness of the British, rejecting corrupt practices that had been in place under the East India Company, administering justice and settling disputes instead, while traveling a district on horseback.[37]

---

[32] Planning Commission, Government of India, The New India: Progress through Democracy (New York: Macmillan, 1958), 15.
[33] Ibid.
[34] Ibid.
[35] Ibid., 10.
[36] Ibid., 11-12.
[37] Ibid., 13.

In *Anglo-Indian Attitudes*, Clive Dewey chronicles the life and work of two Britons who dedicated their lives to service in the Indian Civil Service. He begins his work acknowledging it would likely draw criticism from opponents of British colonialism as well as those who believe that the presence of the British benefitted India. Dewey rejects the adoption of either position as legitimate when making judgment of the actions of individuals, choosing to "accept the possibility that ideas driven by the process of intellectual discovery direct our action by invading our minds."[38]

Dewey argues that within the Indian Civil Service were many men, who because of their childhoods, education, training, and actions, had an impact on Indian society that would be foolish for historians to ignore. Since the numbers of years of service for an ICS officer was 35, such men had more than enough time to shape the culture and policy in the areas in which they worked, often ruling over 300,000 people on their own.[39] There was, however, a divide in the ICS, which meant it "veered between...assimilation and preservation...between westernizers who wanted to change Indian and orientalists who loved it..."[40]

By the time India became independent, the 980-strong officer corps had over 500 native officers, many of who continued to serve through their 35-year commitment and beyond. The British ICS left the country, but not without misgivings, as one said in 1946: You want us to leave India. We would leave very soon but one thing you must remember that you would not be able to maintain those vaulting standards of fairness, honesty, efficaciousness and diligence in administration, which we maintained because of the conspicuous role of the ICS and other services despite difficulties of governing and numerous odds faced by us. Time would come when many of you would remember us with tears in your eyes.[41]

Under the crown, particular industries continued to flourish, though the lives of India's poorest did not dramatically change. About 70% of Indians remained agricultural workers. Those who entered businesses, those who grew crops that could be exported, and educated professionals saw great improvement in their economic status.[42] During the Raj, trade in both opium and indigo greatly declined, and new products–such as cotton, jute, iron, and wheat–began to dominate. Though much of what Indians produced brought about profit through export, some of these industries actually blocked out British products, as we will see below.[43]

Before the 1850s, cotton produced in India was largely exported to Europe for spinning or weaving. What was spun in India was completely by hand. The first steam-powered cotton mill did not reach India until 1856. Indians within the industry soon realized that their greatest profits

---

[38] Clive Dewey, *Anglo-Indian Attitudes: Mind of the Indian Civil Service*. (London: The Hambledon Press, 1993), viii.
[39] Ibid., 12.
[40] Ibid., 14.
[41] R.K. Kaushik, "The Men Who Ran the Raj." Hindustan Times. April 17, 2012.
[42] McLeod, 86.
[43] Ibid., 86-87.

could be made not in shipping raw materials to Europe, where it was difficult to compete, but in spinning in the new factories being built in India. The strategy worked. By becoming a leader in mechanized spinning, India beat out British competition and became the major supplier of yarn to China and Japan, as well as leading with 68% of domestic consumption. The addition of power looms in the 1880s meant more of the production process was kept at home. By the early 20th century, cotton textile production had become India's most important industry.[44] Unlike many other industries remaining in British hands, the cotton industry became truly domestic and is the best example of laissez-faire capitalism, which was the operant policy in India after the 1858 transition.[45] Gandhi would later condemn this westernization of India and call for a return to hand-spinning, both as a form of protest and salvation for India.

---

[44] Ibid., 86.
[45] B. B. Misra, The Indian Middle Classes: Their Growth in Modern Times (London: Oxford University Press, 1961), 215.

Gandhi

Railroad construction in India had begun before the Raj in 1850, and the first train operated in 1853.[46] The milestone of passenger transport was marked with great celebration as the British expressed the hope that "a well-designed system of Railways, ably and prudently executed, would be the most powerful of all worldly instruments of the advancement of civilization in every respect."[47] By 1861, there were over 1500 miles of railroad track completed. This number would be well over 40,000 miles by the late 1950s.[48] In his study of economic improvements under the Raj, I.D. Derbyshire, who rejects what he calls the "immiserationist" interpretation of

---

[46] Ian Kerr., *Engines of Change: The Railroads that Made India.* (Westport, Connecticut: Praeger, 2007), 5.
[47] Ibid., 6.
[48] Ibid., 10.

the Raj. He also argues that recent scholarship tends to support a "meliorist," or positive, view of British rule.[49] Derbyshire cites three factors in the improvement of Indian life and per capita income growth for the native population: a peaceful and well-administered government after 1857; the expansion of European markets for raw goods and easier access to these markets through technology; and the development of India's rail system.[50] The railways constructed in India brought many benefits, including commercial reliability. Rail helped to alleviate the effects of monsoon rains on trade prior to rail travel. Though weather affected trains, the flow of commerce was steadier during the days of land and river transport, and they could be shut down completely at times. River and land transport also faced challenges as a result of changes being wrought in India. Though riverboat carriage was the cheapest form of transport for goods, it was also "risky, seasonal…and excruciatingly slow."[51] These problems were exacerbated by the effects of canal building in India which lowered river levels and made transport of goods by river even more challenging in certain areas. Land transport via pack animals improved after the innovation of the bullock cart, but faced challenges similar to those of the riverboat.

"The most magnificent railway station in the world." says the caption of the stereographic tourist picture of Victoria Terminus, Bombay, which was completed in 1888.

Railway construction would change the Indian economy radically and permanently, especially in Western India. Railways provided a vital link between India's fertile and heavily populated Doabs (regions of great agricultural yield due to rich soils and heavy cultivation) and the port cities of Bombay and Karachi.[52] Though Indian nationalist writers often claimed the changes wrought by rail were responsible for the famines that periodically struck India during the Raj,

---

[49] Derbyshire, I. D. "Economic Change and the Railways in North India, 1860-1914." *Modern Asian Studies* 21, no. 3 (1987): 522.
[50] Ibid., 523.
[51] Ibid., 526.
[52] Ibid., 527.

Derbyshire rejects their claim that agricultural production shifted from grains and subsistence farming to a singular focus on cash crops for exports such as sugar, indigo, and cotton. Instead, he claims rail and the accompanying lower shipping rates, as well as the opening of the Doabs to western ports, allowed production of both domestically consumed grains and cash crops to increase "in tandem."[53] Grain production, he states, actually increased, from 57,000 tons in the years between 1880-1884 to over 560,000 tons in the years prior to World War I. While some of the increase was shipped overseas to newly opened export markets, over 300,000 tons of grain during this period were shipped inward and consumed domestically.[54] Grain production was mixed with the production of crops that helped to restore the soil and allow for year-round production.

Rail also changed the traditional practices of Indian rural areas. It had been common practice for villages to build grain storage facilities and to store up the excess for protection against crop failures. While this storage had often saved lives in earlier times, the implementation of cheap rail transport made this type of grain storage obsolete. Grain could go immediately to market to meet the demand, and where disaster struck, rail allowed a targeted response. Comparing two periods of short supply, the 1860 crop failures (when rail access was still limited), saw famine conditions even with a transport of 175,000 tons of grain to affected areas. Similar conditions in 1907 were alleviated with 725,000 tons of grain shipped by rail.[55]

While Derbyshire's work rejects the overall claim that the rich grew richer and the poor grew poorer as a result of the Raj and rail, he concedes that the development of West Indian farming led to a decline for agricultural workers in the East. At the same time, he notes that rail benefitted eastern regions by creating cheap transportation opportunities for East Indian workers who found employment in the Jute mills.

The number of people who were transported by rail in India grew each year. In 1920, 175 million Indians traveled by train somewhere in the country.[56] The railroad also became one of the three largest employers of the Indian population, just behind the Indian Army, the post, and telegraph. Today, the railroad continues to employ 1.6 million Indians.[57]

British innovations, particularly in rail, Derbyshire claims, were not the direct cause of the negative impact nationalist writers often claim. While those critical of the Raj's impact would cite slowed population growth, famine, decreased native land holdings, and the decline of the handicraft industry as evidence, more recent scholarship indicates these problems were more localized and offset by gains in other areas. Though both sides would agree the more

---

[53] Ibid., 530.
[54] Ibid.
[55] Ibid., 532.
[56] Ritika Prasad., *Tracks of Change: Railways and Everyday Life in Colonial India.* (Daryaganj: Cambridge University Press, 2015) 2.
[57] Kartar Lalvani, 21.

independent, middle-class farmers and upper classes benefitted much more and at a faster rate than the poorest agricultural workers, meliorists claim the negative impact of rail was the result of already existing poor hygiene which spread more quickly and easily as a result of rail transport. Derbyshire cites Gandhi on the matter, recalling his statement regarding "the protection of natural segregation was trenched upon and India was opened up to a scourge of disease such as South America had been in the 16th century."[58] He reminds his readers that cyclical famine as a result of crop failures was a part of Indian life, well before British rule, and in fact, that the impact of famine was greatly reduced post-1900 by the very existence of rail.

Of the four charges nationalist historians hold against the British, Derbyshire credits one: the decline of the handicraft industry. As far as the other charges, he exhorts the student of Indian history to consider the economic motives of the writers who were often the best-educated Indian natives, hailing from Bengal. It was, Derbyshire contends, the opening of prosperity to those in the lower classes and castes that influenced these writers to view the continuing changes as harmful. Having experienced the benefits of favorable relations with the British East India Company, they were loath to see opportunities open to all of India and not just to a select few. Additionally, Derbyshire calls his readers' attention to the conditions under which critical writing was undertaken, pointing out that during times of famine (in works he calls "gloomy"), the conclusions of nationalists were far more condemning of the British than during times of prosperity.[59]

In the final assessment of the benefits of British rail and accompanying economic change during the Raj, Derbyshire insists the division between those who condemn the Raj as negative and those who believe it benefitted India, results primarily, not from a difference in the data considered, but in the question asked. For nationalists, the question is: "Why did India not achieve takeoff?" asked in light of "their disappointment with comparative growth and income trends between India and Europe." For "meliorists," the question is instead: "Did per capita income rise between 1860 and 1920?"[60] He suggests that a middle ground, recognizing both significant growth and the limitations of that growth compared to other parts of the world, provides the most accurate accounting.[61]

For all the accomplishments of the Raj, many British and Indians alike offered criticism of the British policy in India. This critique did not always accuse the British of bringing no improvements to India, but instead, pointed out that the benefits that did come with the East India Company, and later with direct rule, were beneficial primarily to Westerners. In the short-term, many local artisans and craftspeople were put out of business, but in the long term, critics said, the harm was far more devastating, resulting in long-term poverty and destructive patterns.

---

[58] Derbyshire., 539.
[59] Ibid., 543.
[60] Ibid., 544.
[61] Ibid.

Romesh Dutt, a Calcutta-born 26-year member of the Indian Civil Service, was educated in the West. Like so many exposed to a Western education, he eventually critiqued the very system that had employed him, and resigned his position to become a voice for Indian independence.[62] He commended the British for their contributions, which he lists as peace, Western education, a strong administrative government, and a pure justice system,[63] calling these "results which no honest critic of British rule in India regards without high admiration."[64] Nevertheless, Dutt offers much critique for Britain's economic approach in India, arguing, "it is, unfortunately, true that the East India Company and the British Parliament, following the selfish commercial policy of a hundred years ago, discouraged Indian manufacturers in the early years of British rule in order to encourage the rising manufactures of England."[65] Dutt criticizes the British in three areas: their trade policies–which "crippled" India's manufacturing; their impressive, yet devastating, collection of a land tax; and their demand for interest on the debt owed by India to the mother country as a result of the 1857 rebellion.[66]

Another Indian writer, Kartar Lalvani, has written a book that seeks to defend Britain's record in India. As a 50-year resident of England, Lalvani claims to have been unable to find a single Brit who would name a positive aspect of the British governance of India. Without denying that Britain was guilty–as many other nations have been–of exploiting India for her wealth, Lalvani's perspective is that once the country passed out of the hands of the British East India company and directly to the Crown, the contributions were positive and should be judged fairly.[67] He states, "The indisputable fact is that India, as a nation as it stands today, was originally created by a small, isolated island nation. India has endured as a democracy and as a unified nation thanks to the all-important and fully functional infrastructure of an independent civil service and judiciary, a disciplined and apolitical army and a well-drilled and efficient police force, all developed by the imperial power. Of course, the labor was local, indeed skillful, and the indigenous cultures were ancient and sophisticated, but it is worth pausing to consider what India would be like today if the British had chosen to stay at home."[68]

Author of *Indian Tales of the Raj*, Zareer Masani, describes his encounters with those who had lived through the British occupation period. Many of them bristle at what they saw as the British "obsession" with the Raj period, believing that other periods and influences are a more significant story for modern India. Thankfully, Masani pressed forward to record the remembrances of those who had lived through the period, whether highly critical of the British administration, cooperative, or in strong support.[69]

---

[62] Romett Dutt in Martin Deming Lewis, 1.
[63] Ibid.
[64] Ibid.
[65] Ibid., 2.
[66] Ibid., 5.
[67] John Preston, "The British Were Imperialist Brutes? No, Britain Made India Great (says an Indian)". UK Daily Mail, 17 March 2016.
[68] Kartar Lalvani, *The Making of India: The Untold Story of British Enterprise*. (London: Bloomsbury Continuum, 2016), 2.

In 1885, only four years before the birth of Jawaharlal Nehru, the Indian National Congress organized and began the path to Indian independence. Still in its infant stages, the Congress would not see its goal complete until 1947. The Congress and the young man who would come to dominate it endured a long journey, fraught with delays and opposition, until he became India's first independent prime minister.

In its early stages, the Congress acted as a training ground for India's newly educated and politically awakened young men to hone their leadership skills. Meeting initially during the Christmas season, they passed a series of resolutions for change in India's governance, demanding "greater access by Indians to positions of governmental power, fewer taxes, reductions in military expenditure, and compulsory elementary education."[70] Although the resolutions coming out of the Congress were often ignored by British officials, "India's new young leaders-in-embryo…learned from their early failures how better to appeal for justice, equality of opportunity, and fair play–British ideals they culled from the works of Milton, Macaulay, Mill, and Morley, which they memorized and articulated more eloquently than most British officials."[71]

Jawaharlal Nehru was born into a well-off Indian family and educated at English boarding schools, where he received a classical education along with many of his contemporaries. While at Harrow, he was exposed to a biography of the Italian nationalist Garibaldi, a figure who captured his imagination and admiration.[72] His later admiration of the Irish Independence movement caused Nehru to come into conflict with his moderate father, who had put great stock in the Raj early on, and enjoyed the benefits of British favor.[73] His son, having graduated from Cambridge and studying to pass the barrister's exam, eventually embraced a similar lifestyle in London, despite his attraction to the more radical elements of the Indian independence movement and a growing resentment of discrimination, which he regularly experienced at University.[74]

---

[69] Zareer Masani, Indian Tales of the Raj. (Berkeley: University of California Press, 1987), 1-6.
[70] Stanley Wolpert, "A Mixed Legacy: From the Raj to Modern India," Harvard International Review 32, no. 4 (2011).
[71] Ibid.
[72] Benjamin Zachariah, Nehru (New York: Routledge, 2004), 17.
[73] Ibid., 21.
[74] Ibid., 27.

Nehru

In 1912, upon his return to India to begin practicing law with his father, the Swadeshi movement was already well underway. Swadeshi, meaning "of our own country," encouraged the forsaking of British goods and the colonial lifestyle, a movement that Nehru's family rejected. Instead, his father purchased a British automobile, marking himself as a man interested in continued cooperation and loyalty to the British way of life, in the mind of his son. Nevertheless, Nehru remained a faithful son, marrying a Brahmin girl in a match arranged by his father.[75]

Nehru remained interested in Indian independence, and resented what he saw as the divide and conquer methods employed by the British—emphasizing the enmity between Muslim and Hindu populations and helping to form the Muslim League, which would fight for its own rights, rather than for the recognition of Indian rights as a whole. The 1916 Lucknow Pact, signed by both the Muslim League and the National Congress, brought Hindus and Muslims together, as well as helping to promote cooperation between the two opposing independence parties, one more

---

[75] Ibid., 28.

radical, the other more moderate, in its demands for home rule.

It was there, at the Lucknow Conference, that Nehru first met Mahatma Gandhi. Gandhi had returned to India from South Africa in 1915, where he had campaigned for better treatment of Indian soldiers stationed there by the British.[76] After spending a year touring India, Gandhi began his non-cooperation movement, encouraging civil disobedience, specifically appealing to Indian peasants through his peasant dress and manner of speaking.[77] Nehru's biographer, Benjamin Zechariah, notes that at the time of their Lucknow meeting, Nehru was "unable…to relate to [Gandhi's} style."[78] Though Nehru's father had joined the independence movement (largely as a result of British persecution of those who called for it), the Nehrus believed the path to Indian independence lay in the hands of the upper-middle, educated class, not in embracing the cause of Indian peasants or support of the British during WWI.[79]

India supported the British and her victorious allies during WWI, sending 1.5 million soldiers to war, funded with Indian revenue. During the war, progress was made in domestic industry and many British exports were disrupted. These factors led many to believe that Britain would now take its promises regarding India's independence seriously. Despite some action–such as the Montagu-Chelmsford reforms, which moderates believed held hope for the future–many Indians believed that "the British were willing to leave India–but always tomorrow."[80] The British agreed to further training for Indian nationalists, but also claimed their immediate removal would lead to conflict between the Muslims and Hindus and a vacuum of power in the East that would destabilize the world.

Along with reform and cooperation, the British became increasingly dedicated to putting down the radicals who demanded a timetable they were unwilling to give. This was to be accomplished, in part, by extending the Rowlatt Bills, allowing martial law in India during the war.

Gandhi responded by launching his first Indian Satyagraha,[81] a tactic he had used successfully in South Africa. The movement encouraged Indians to "court arrest,"[82] an idea Nehru also embraced, though his father did not. Father and son would be divided in their agreement over the tactics employed in pursuing justice for India. Gandhi's methods, in fact, continued to confuse the more established independence movement. The head of the Muslim League, Muhammad Ali Jinnah, also protested the Rowlatt Bills, but both the Muslims and Hindus in Congress believed "Gandhi's 'extreme program' attracted the inexperienced and the illiterate, and caused further

---

[76] Ibid., 33.
[77] Stanley Wolpert.
[78] Zechariah, 33.
[79] Ibid., 33-4.
[80] Ibid., 35.
[81] Stanley Wolpert, Gandhi's Passion: The Life and Legacy of Mahatma Gandhi (New York: Oxford University Press, 2002), 99.
[82] Zechariah, 36.

division everywhere in the country."[83]

Gandhi called for a rejection of British custom, including the burning of all British clothing, a boycott of British goods, and the unity of Muslims and Hindus in the fight to repeal the Rowlatt laws. He advised his followers to conduct their protest openly and without resistance to arrest, believing the appeal to right and justice, rather than violence, would win the day. Gandhi's methods were considered both dangerous and offensive by many British officials, including Winston Churchill, who believed that any willingness on the part of the British government to negotiate with Gandhi would be interpreted as weakness. Churchill was offended by what he believed was a deliberate deception by the man he referred to as a "seditious middle Temple lawyer"[84] to engage the support of the Indian people against British rule: "Gandhi, with deep knowledge of the Indian peoples, by the dress he wore—or did not wear, by the way in which his food was brought to him at the Vice regal Palace, deliberately insulted, in a manner which he knew everyone in India would appreciate, the majesty of the King's representative. These are not trifles in the East. Thereby our power to maintain peace and order among the immense masses of India has been sensibly impaired."[85]

---

[83] Wolpert, Gandhi's passion, 100.
[84] Ramachandra Guha, "Churchill and Gandhi", The Hindu Magazine. June 19, 2005.
[85] Ibid.

Churchill in the early 20th century

Gandhi's April 1919 arrest led to heightened tensions in India as violence broke out in response. Though Gandhi rejected the violence on his behalf as a violation of satyagraha, the British continued to see resistance to the Rowlatt laws and developed a growing fear of Indian revolt.

On April 13, in one of the biggest turning points in India's history, a gathering of unarmed celebrants at Amritsar, or Jallianwala Bagh, was fired upon by British soldiers under the command of Reginald Dyer. Over 400 were killed.[86] As the details of the massacre were

---

[86] Stanley Wolpert, Gandhi's Passion, 101.

discovered (initially Gandhi himself blamed the Punjabis and tended to believe the British were in the right), the event "effectively killed moderate opinion in India."[87]

Gandhi in 1919

Nehru turned to socialism as the liberating force for India, while Gandhi retreated to semi-seclusion to restore himself both physically and spiritually. Frustrated and angry at the delay in progress, Nehru angrily wrote to Gandhi: "What then can be done? You say nothing—you only criticize and no helpful lead comes from you."[88] Nehru's ultimate rejection of the non-violence movement and full conversion to communism was soon to come. Gandhi's biographer explains: "To hold such an idealist as young Nehru in check Gandhi knew that he would have to abandon his life of rural retreat, returning first to the hurly-burly of urban political chaos like that he had

---

[87] Zachariah, 38.
[88] Stanley Wolpert, *Gandhi's Passion.*, 129.

found so hateful in Calcutta, and then to the enforced solitude of long years behind British bars and barbed wire walls."[89]

Nehru had no faith in hand spinning, or the return to simpler and less Western times Gandhi advocated. He also considered Gandhi's ancient Hindu ideals outdated and impractical, if not reactionary. But by the end of the decade, Gandhi emerged once again, hoping to save India from Nehru's now-communist leanings (despite their sometimes strained friendship) and accomplish independence in both a political and spiritual sense.

The Hindu-Muslim Divide

"Long years ago, we made a tryst with destiny and now the time comes when we shall redeem our pledge." – Jawaharlal Nehru

The origins of the Hindu-Muslim antipathy in India can be traced to the original entry of Muslim invaders into the sub-continent, and comparisons have often been made to the arrival of the Muslims in India and the later arrival of the British. Unlike earlier migrations of Aryans and Kushans, from whom were drawn the fundamental elements of Indian Hindu society, both the British and the various Muslim waves remained aloof and culturally exclusive. The British, of course, never claimed to be Indian and retained the advantage of a separate homeland, while the Muslims chose to integrate to the extent that they claimed the subcontinent as a homeland, but at the same time adopted a separate identity.

German diplomat Wilhelm von Pochhammer, who served extensively in India and wrote widely on Indian politics and history, made essentially this observation in his book *India's Road to Nationhood*, published first in 1981 and which remains today one of the most impartial and reliable accounts of the era. "The Central Asiatic Moslems," Pochhammer wrote, "who came to India had no homeland. They were forced to look upon conquered land as their new homeland, although each day showed them that for the mass of the subjugated people they remained foreigners."

The Muslims — if such an observation were to be accepted, and it is certainly not by any means universally accepted — played the role of a governing aristocracy, aloof from the masses and separated by their religious exclusivity and their foreign origins. They were never absolute aliens, like the British, but they were never Indians. They were also driven by the missionary zeal, so common among Abrahamic religions, to convert the masses to their own faith, and such an attitude immediately implies an imperviousness to any reciprocating adaption. History, of course, would prove that India's Islamic invaders failed to convert the mass of Hindus to Islam, achieving at the very best an accommodation within India for a Muslim minority.

---

[89] Wolpert, 133.

With the arrival of the British, however, power was gradually transferred from Muslim to Anglo/Christian hands. Initially, therefore, the Muslim ruling elite resented the gradual British takeover, while it was generally embraced by the Hindus, for whom it meant liberation from Muslim domination. To India, Britain introduced Western education and modernization, which tended to favor the development of Hindu elites more than Muslim. The concept of the "Indian Renaissance" is generally understood to have come about thanks to these influences. Indian reformer and revivalist Raja Rammohan Roy was one of the earliest propagators of modern Western education, seeing it as a powerful instrument for the spread of modern ideas in India. He was associated with the foundation the Hindu College in Calcutta (which later came to be known as the Presidency College). He also maintained at his own cost an English school in Calcutta and, in addition, established Vedanta College, where both Indian learning and courses in Western social and physical science were offered.

That is not to say that Muslim leaders did not recognize a need to compete in this regard. One such was Syed Ahmad bin Muttaqi Khan KCSI, more commonly known as Sir Syed. Syed Khan was an Indian Muslim "pragmatist", Islamic reformist, and philosopher of nineteenth-century British India. He too recognized the advantageous elements of British rule, establishing such prestigious institutions as the Mohamedan Anglo-Oriental College, founded in 1875, which later emerged as Aligarh Muslim University.

This institution in due course became the seedbed of the parallel "Muslim Renaissance", which refused to ally itself with the "Indian Renaissance" insofar as it was dominated by Hindus, urging instead a wider embrace and appreciation of Islam. He went on to found the Muslim Educational Council, the Indian Patriotic Association, and the Mohammedan Defense Association of Upper India. Clearly, Sir Syed, alongside his reform agenda, championed the notion of a separate Muslim identity.

The 1858 arrival of Imperial Britain in India, while igniting this parallel movement, was also quick to recognize the potential of playing one off against the other to its own advantage. This, a tried and tested British imperial strategy, aided each individual community's march toward modernity, while at the same time stirring up the latent residue of their mutual loathing.

The Muslim portion of the Bengali population generally welcomed the partition of the territory into east and west, recognizing the immediate precedent that this established for separate territorial cantons. Lord Curzon pleaded publicly that the move was strictly administrative, but even if this was so, the message that it sent was clear enough. The British were prepared to tolerate territorial separation, and so a two-state solution was feasible.

This tacit approval was soon afterward codified into law with a series of constitutional reforms undertaken in 1909, known as the Morley-Minto Reforms. During the framing of these reforms, Sir Sultan Muhammed Shah, the Aga Khan, put pressure on the British government for a separate Muslim electorate, which was acknowledged and accepted and included in the Act of

1909. If Lord Curzon's partition of Bengal provided the precedent, the constitutional reforms of 1909 established that precedent in law. The extension of this to actually putting forward a geographic area as a potential Muslim state was achieved consequent to a second series of constitutional reforms under the chairmanship of Sir John Allsebrook Simon, who arrived in British-occupied India in 1928. As Sir John Simon's took evidence, the League proposed the provinces of Sind and Baluchistan, both now a province of Pakistan, as separate Muslim territories. This proposition was not adopted by the commission, and no one really thought that it would, but names had nonetheless been mentioned and aspirations ventilated, and for the time being, that was enough.

It has often been remarked that India was created by the British, and certainly, it was the British that combined the multiple kingdoms and fiefdoms of the sub-continent into a single nation, and it was opposition to the continuation of British rule and a common determination of overthrow it that united that nation. At the same time, an unfortunate feature of Indian political development during the early 20th century was the inability of Congress (and the Indian nationalist movement in general) to attract the participation of the Muslim minority. For this, many reasons were offered, including the Islamic view of cow-killing, language exclusivities, a conspicuous Muslim alliance with the British, and perhaps even a movement among Muslims at the time. All of this suggested that Islam differed from Hinduism in its compatibility with Western values and thinking, and these explanations sought to account for a seemingly enduring and suppurating antipathy that had endured for centuries and which simply would not heal.

By the late 19th century, however, the longevity of this division had almost nothing to do with conventions of religion, education, or modern thinking, and everything to do with politics. At the root of it lay a Muslim fear of domination by Hindus, if the Hinducentric Congress sought to position itself as the sole representative of the nation. It was self-evident to the Muslim minority leadership that the Indian Muslim community, in general, could not hope to prevail under democratic rules quite as it had under the British, and thus exclusivity and communalism began increasingly to inform Muslim political rhetoric.

The British, meanwhile, exacerbated this resurgent hostility between Hindus and Muslims when the decision was made in 1905 to partition the eastern province of Bengal.[90] This was ordered by the then Viceroy of India, Lord Curzon, ostensibly to improve administrative efficiency, but in practical terms, it was to separate Muslims and Hindus in a region of India where populations were somewhat even and where communal violence was commonplace and growing. Hindus, of course, saw this as an extension of the British divide-and-rule policy, which was not wholly untrue, while Muslims saw it as the first tacit acknowledgement by the British that separation was the only solution.

---

[90] The Partition of Bengal divided the provincial state of Bengal into predominantly Hindu West Bengal and the predominantly Muslim East Bengal. East Bengal would form the basis of East Pakistan and later the independent state of Bangladesh.

It was around this event that Muslim separatism first began to find expression. In the East Bengali capital of Dhaka, a year after partition, the All-India Muslim League was founded as the voice of the Muslim minority. Obviously, the time and location of this must be viewed in the context of the partition, and notwithstanding protestations to the contrary, the formation of the Muslim League was an unmistakable precursor to Muslim pleas for separation. Like Congress, the early political temper of the Muslim League, or simply the League, was moderate and conservative, but despite this, its mere formation sowed the seeds of communalism in the wider political discourse of India, setting the Muslim minority on a separate political course.

In the 1910s, Muhammad Ali Jinnah represented the Muslim facet of the Indian independence movement, and like Nehru and Gandhi, he was a British-trained lawyer.[91] He was Muslim, of a minority faction, and of comparatively humble background. He was a spare and aesthetic man, more generous in his opinion of the British, and generally, he stood apart from the likes of Gandhi and Nehru in his willingness to collaborate and cooperate. The minority status of Muslims in India tended to soften Muslim attitudes towards the British, insofar as it was under British, secular rule that the Muslims were protected from inevitable numerical domination by Hindus. Jinnah served on the Imperial Legislative Council and was a Congress member, but he stood somewhat in the "unity" camp. He was initially opposed to the formation of the All-India Muslim League, taking the position that any principle of separate electorates simply served to divide the nation.

---

[91] Nehru was significantly senior in both caste and professional attributes to both Gandhi and Jinnah. His secondary education was completed at Harrow, second only to Eton as the most prestigious British private school, from where he gained entry to Trinity College Cambridge, equally prestigious.

Jinnah and Gandhi

While remaining a member of Congress, Jinnah joined the Muslim League in 1913, although he continued to serve and stand as the principal Muslim voice in Congress. In 1916, however, he was elected to the presidency of the Muslim League, with now a foot in both camps, and in that capacity, he was instrumental in negotiating the terms of the Lucknow Pact. The Lucknow Pact was an important agreement between the two parties that undertook to increase pressure on the British for greater Indian representation and to establish quotas for Hindu and Muslim representation on the various councils and committees that were open to Indian participation.

During World War I, Jinnah stood on the "dominion" platform, which preceded the Purna Swaraj movement with the demand that India be granted the same dominion status as the white colonies. In this regard, he suffered the same general disillusion as other Indian nationalist leaders as they reeled under the effects of the Jallianwala Bagh Massacre after World War I. Like many Muslims, he was depressed by the collapse of the Ottoman Empire and the disempowerment of the Ottoman caliphate. It all tended to compound a sense in his mind that the tide of history was tipping away from Indian Muslims and toward Indian Hindus.

As a lawyer and a constitutionalist, Jinnah instinctively opposed Gandhi, disturbed by the extra-constitutional nature of non-cooperation and satyagraha. His relationship with Gandhi (and vice versa) would always be chilly and restrained, and the two never managed to muster any real affection for one another. He remained publicly cordial toward Gandhi, however, no doubt recognizing the folly of swimming against a tide of popular adoration for the Mahatma among both impoverished Hindus and Muslims.

After the war, Jinnah sought to distance himself from both Congress and the League. He resigned from Congress and passed most of the 1920s away from the center of the Indian political stage. In his absence, the independence movement continued to gather momentum, quite as British opposition to it continued to solidify. Winston Churchill, always an influential voice of the British conservative movement, bitterly opposed any suggestion of Indian independence, and his personal antipathy toward Gandhi found expression in his usual acerbic wit, for which he has since become universally famous. The "half-naked fakir," Churchill opined, "ought best to be bound hand and foot and crushed by an elephant ridden by the viceroy."[92]

The essence of Churchill's opposition to Indian independence or any move toward it was the impoverishment within Britain that would follow the removal of India from the British economic equation. The 1929 British general election, however, removed the Conservative government of Stanley Baldwin from office, and it also removed Winston Churchill from the cabinet office of Chancellor of the Exchequer. The government was replaced with the Labor administration of Ramsay MacDonald. The MacDonald administration, by definition more liberal than the previous Conservative government, was nonetheless influenced by the same general forces. Various round table conferences and fact-finding missions sought in vain to find that elusive formula that would satisfy Indian nationalist fervor and at the same time require Britain to relinquish no actual political control.

Meanwhile, the 1930s dawned, and an increasingly defiant and maturing Congress raised the tricolor flag of independent India on the banks of the Ravi River in Lahore, defining the future direction of the movement. A month later, on January 26, 1930, Congress issued a declaration of sovereignty and self-rule, or Purna Swaraj, implicit in which was a stated readiness to withhold taxes as part of a revival of Gandhi's campaign of civil disobedience.

A Congress working committee then authorized Gandhi to put this declaration into effect by organizing the first orchestrated, Congress-sanctioned act of civil disobedience. Gandhi, as was his habit, meditated deeply on this. The most obvious and generally deplored British tax then in effect was the 1882 Salt Tax, which underwrote an official government monopoly on salt production by banning the traditional, communal production of salt. Violation of the Salt Act was a criminal offense, and Gandhi chose a mass violation of the British salt laws as the vehicle for his national satyagraha.

---

[92] The context of this comment was a meeting of the West Essex Conservative Association, specially convened so that Churchill could explain his position. He remarked: "...It is alarming and also nauseating to see Mr Gandhi, a seditious Middle Temple lawyer, now posing as a fakir of a type well known in the East, striding half-naked up the steps of the Vice-regal palace ... to parley on equal terms with the representative of the King-Emperor.'

Initially, neither Congress nor the British took the notion of passive resistance centered on salt particularly seriously, but as a point of issue, it satisfied Gandhi's typical preference for simplicity, as well as touching to the heart of the petty and mean-spirited nature of British monopolistic legislation. Indians were legally disallowed from utilizing the universal resource of the sea to produce salt and were instead required to purchase it, contributing thus a tax revenue that affected the poorest Indians most acutely.

It took very little to stoke popular outrage, and Gandhi, with his flair for the theatrical and a very shrewd history of using the popular press, began to do just that. He added to a building anticipation in the countryside by issuing regular declamations against the British, and his public meditations and performances proved emotive and enormously influential. His satyagraha would take the form of a march.

The concept of a "march" had been accidentally arrived at in South Africa, during a series of Indian labor strikes and had proved in practice to be wildly successful. It had popular appeal and held the potential to gather momentum over an extended period. Gandhi set off from his Sabarmati Ashram in rural Gujarat on March 12, 1930 at the head of a small entourage of followers, intending to walk the 240 miles to the coastal village of Dandi in order to symbolically contravene the law by producing a small amount of salt.

By the time he reached Dandi and boiled a pot of seawater, he was surrounded by an entourage of some 50,000 people. This number, however, was dwarfed by the subsequent mass civil disobedience movement that swept the country. Millions broke the salt laws by manufacturing or purchasing illegal salt. British cloth and numerous other manufactured goods were boycotted, and many similar laws were overtly broken. Some 60,000 arrests were made. Violence broke out in a great many places, but this time Gandhi, aside from appealing for an end to it, did not suspend the action. Several sub-marches were mounted, one by a Muslim Pashto disciple of Gandhi, Ghaffar Khan, in the province of Peshwar, which resulted in troops firing on protesters, killing upward of 200. Indeed, a platoon of the Royal Garhwal Rifles refused, in the end, orders to fire on the crowd.

It was an unprecedented event on a national scale that shook the British administration to its core. Gandhi was arrested, and without charge or trial, he was jailed. Nine months later, however, fearing a popular reaction, he was released unconditionally, and soon afterward, what was known as the Gandhi-Irwin Pact (Lord Irwin was then Viceroy of India) was signed. This essentially committed the British government to negotiate a path toward self-government, and the result of this was the Government of India Act of 1935, a partial roadmap to Indian independence. Although the act committed the British government to make many authentic concessions to Indian demands, it nonetheless fell short of an actual grant of independence.

Despite this, it was a huge step in the right direction, including the grant of limited franchise to millions of Indians. The three major provisions, however, included the establishment of a loose federal structure, achieving a degree of provincial autonomy, and safeguarding minority interests through separate electorates.

In 1937, the act came into effect, although without its federal provisions, thanks primarily to opposition from rulers of the Princely States. An election, however, was held that, although of limited political impact since it offered Indians nominal administrative positions well away from the executive, did reveal one important fact. The ballot was dominated by Congress, while the All-India Muslim League returned a generally disappointing result. If the Muslim minority feared being overwhelmed at the ballot by the Hindu majority, then this proved that it would likely be so. It was now time for action.

In 1939, the Governor-General, without consultation, committed India to Imperial and Allied defense in World War II. This had the twin effect of pitching the recently empowered provisional authorities into rebellion, but also it galvanized the Muslim League to act. Muhammad Ali Jinnah, who was by then president of the League, persuaded participants at the 1940 annual congress of the party, held in Lahore, to adopt what later came to be known as the Lahore Resolution. This, in its simplest terms, demanded the division of India into two separate sovereign states — one Muslim, the other Hindu. This was the first definitive articulation of what later came to known as the Two Nation Theory. Although the notion of Pakistan as a separate state had been under discussion from as early as 1930, it had gained very little currency. However, a renewed antipathy between Hindus and Muslims in the aftermath of provincial elections breathed new life into the idea, and once it found expression at a national level, it more or less became de facto.

Congress, under the leadership of Jawaharlal Nehru, naturally rejected the principal of separate electorates outright, maintaining its claim of the only universal, authentic representative of all Indians. There were only two powers in India, Nehru claimed: Congress and the British government.

Planning the Partition

"We have undoubtedly achieved Pakistan, and that too without bloody war, practically peacefully, by moral and intellectual force, and with the power of the pen, which is no less mighty than that of the sword and so our righteous cause has triumphed." - Jinnah

In 1933, Muslim nationalist Choudhry Rahmat Ali created the hybrid name "Pakistan", further drawing a circle around the northern provinces of India. The name was created by taking "P" from Punjab, "A" from Afghanistan (which was then the North West Frontier Province), "K" from Kashmir, "S" from Sind and "tan" from Baluchistan — no clearer articulation that this was required to illustrate the scope of the future autonomous Muslim territory.

To a large extent, the widening gap between the two Indian nationalist parties was the product of the difference in personalities between Gandhi, Nehru, and Jinnah. Gandhi resigned from Congress in 1934, for reasons he explained as an unwillingness to be associated with certain Congress policies and for what he saw as indiscipline in the ranks of the party. Others have suggested that his eccentric style of politics and activism was simply no longer compatible with a party preparing practical strategies for an exchange of power. It is also perhaps true that Gandhi's growing popularity and charisma competed uncomfortably with the public profiles of more than one influential leader of Congress. One such was Jawaharlal Nehru, who was perhaps closest to the British insofar as his father was a Privy Counsellor, and he himself was very much a product of the British establishment. His father had conditioned him for rule, and he was certainly first in line for the Indian nationalist throne.

In this regard, Indian partition has increasingly in recent years been portrayed as a dual between two individuals fixated on personal power. Gandhi had no interest in power, and so the other individual was Jinnah. Due to his actions as a spoiler, he is often cast as the villain. Jinnah certainly did take an enigmatic position, championing first Indian unity and then distorting that position increasingly to a point when he would consider or hear nothing but partition. Jinnah would achieve partition, but he would never gain the same political heights enjoyed by Nehru and would, perhaps justly, carry the burden of blame for the disaster that followed.

The journey toward the goal of partition continued on March 23, 1940, with the Muslim League announcement of the Lahore Resolution, known also as the Pakistan Resolution. This would prove to be the final, definitive statement of Muslim League intention to pursue the two-state solution. A day before the resolution was published, Jinnah delivered a detailed address to an assembled audience of Muslim League members, clear in its implications and which stated in part, "Musalmans are a nation according to any definition of a nation, and they must have their homeland, their territory and their state."

Jinnah then went on to add, "It is extremely difficult to appreciate why our Hindu friends fail to understand the real nature of Islam and Hinduism. They are not religions in the strict sense of the word, but are, in fact, different and distinct social orders; and it is a dream that the Hindus and Muslims can ever evolve a common nationality; and this misconception of one Indian nation has gone far beyond the limits and is the cause of more of our troubles and will lead India to destruction if we fail to revise our notions in time. The Hindus and Muslims belong to two different religious philosophies, social customs, and literature[s]. They neither intermarry nor interdine together, and indeed they belong to two different civilizations which are based mainly on conflicting ideas and conceptions. Their aspects [perspectives] on life, and of life, are different. It is quite clear that Hindus and Mussalmans derive their inspiration from different sources of history. They have different epics, their heroes are different, and different episode[s]. Very often the hero of one is a foe of the other, and likewise their victories and defeats overlap. To yoke together two such nations under a single state, one as a numerical minority and the other as a majority, must lead to growing discontent, and final. destruction of any fabric that may be so built up for the government of such a state."

Thereafter, the matter of the two-state solution assumed less the aspect of a suggestion than a negotiation. Now that the concept was embedded in the popular consciousness, the question simply became one of establishing practical steps toward it. On July 1, 1940, Jinnah presented a series of proposals to the British government, known as the "Tentative Proposals of Jinnah". These were indeed tentative and said very little about anything, other than perhaps that no successful constitutional strategy for disengagement would be possible without Muslim consent, and Muslim consent would be granted to no solution that fell short of two nations.

Naturally, Britain was entirely consumed by the war effort in 1940, especially the necessity of defending the British Isles from direct German invasion in what has since come to known as the Battle of Britain. Metropolitan Britain was in no position to deal with difficult issues in India, and in practical terms, all other matters were subordinated to the British fight for survival. Once again, however, India would provide a vital bulwark against a German victory in this war, in particular since the Axis powers included Japan this time. The Japanese invasion of Burma, completed in 1942, brought the war to the very borders of India, and Indian compliance in imperial defense was never more vital than now.

It was then that Congress announced its "Quit India" campaign, essentially trading Indian cooperation in the war effort for a firm promise of independence upon an Allied victory. This was a risky move; after all, an Allied defeat would have meant an Axis Victory, which for India would have meant trading Britain as an imperial power for Japan. That would certainly crown Congress's "Quit India" campaign with success, but it might prove to be a pyrrhic victory. The British, however, were in no mood to spar with an opportunistic Congress leadership and clapped the entire top strata in irons, including Gandhi, incarcerating them for the remainder of the war. Congress, therefore, was largely inactive during this period, leaving Jinnah and the Muslim League an open field to cultivate their friendly relations with Britain. It was a poke in the eye for Congress, and Jinnah made the most of it.

Perhaps inevitably, these moves did not silence Indian dissent. Other factors were at play that would prove pivotal in India's journey to independence. Britain was reeling under German attacks, and pleas by Churchill for the United States to enter the war were met by a series of conditions that served to define the terms of the New World Order. One such was the Atlantic Charter, a cornerstone of the United States' view of a changing world. The Atlantic Charter defined Allied post-war objectives, among which were the principles of self-determination, sovereignty, and independence. The British had no choice but to comply with this. The British no longer led the world, and the United States was in favor of Indian independence.

Thus, in March 1942, a senior British cabinet minister (Member of Parliament, Minister of Aircraft Production, and Leader of the House of Commons), Sir Stafford Cripps, arrived in India on a mission to mollify dissent, douse fires among the ranks of Congress, and set the tone for the post-war solution. Trust, however, was entirely absent, and while Cripps offered a virtual blank check on independence at the end of the war, Gandhi, for one, was apt to remark that it was a check drawn on a collapsing bank.

Cripps

Nonetheless, Indian loyalty held during the war, and as Indian manpower mobilized after victory in Europe to drive the Japanese out of Burma, what Cripps had promised appeared in the end to be a self-fulfilling strategy. Winston Churchill won the war, but he did not survive the peace, and the Conservative Party was defeated in the general election of 1945 and replaced by the Labor government of Prime Minister Clement Attlee. Attlee was pro-Indian independence, and almost as soon as he took office, the formal process began.

The Viceroy of India, General Lord Archibald Wavell, was a military man of the North African and South Asian theatres who had little patience with political posturing. He recognized that the

British were finished in India, and so the sooner a British departure could be negotiated, the better. He was also a pragmatist and was prepared to cut through the political bunkum and see the situation for what it was. Congress wished to control a united India, claiming to speak for all Indians, while the Muslim League wished to achieve a two-state solution, ostensibly to protect the religious and cultural exclusivity of Indian Muslims. Behind that was Nehru, poised to assume power, and Jinnah, who wished to lead a nation and not merely a Muslim majority province of a country that Nehru ruled.

Wavell

On September 19, 1945, therefore, Wavell announced that elections to the provincial and central legislatures would be held between December 1945 and January 1946. From the results of this, an executive council would be formed and a constitution-making body convened to take the process forward. This was the first unequivocal British move toward a phased handover of power. In preparation, the British began releasing the leadership of Congress from prison, including Nehru.

The results of the election surprised no one. Congress won more or less every Hindu seat and the Muslim League won every Muslim seat. A few seats here and there went to such parties as the Indian Communist Party, but the overall message was perfectly clear.

In March, following this up, Attlee dispatched a cabinet mission to India to begin negotiating the practical terms of a British handover of power. The mission was headed by Lord Pethick-Lawrence, the Secretary of State for India, Cripps, and A. V. Alexander, the First Lord of the Admiralty. Wavell was present throughout, but he did not participate in negotiations. This was arguably one of the most important British diplomatic missions of the century. It was mounted on the understanding that Indian independence was inevitable and, moreover, that the terms of devolution and the success of the process as a whole would set the tone for what would inevitably be a wider process of decolonization across the former British Empire.

Ideally, the British hoped to retain India within the system of its own defense, even after granting its independence, and thus the British Commonwealth was offered as a future vehicle of common interest. However, the immediate objective was not to be prepared for future wars but to attempt to frame a constitution and establish a constitutional committee and thereafter set up a functioning executive council with bipartisan support from both major parties. At the root of negotiations was the need to establish some sort of power-sharing formula acceptable to both sides. There was about this phase of the mission a certain weary formality, and one can imagine that the likes of Cripps went through the motions in the full and certain knowledge that no such unified India was possible. Muslim fears that the British Raj would simply evolve into the Hindu Raj were not unfounded, and Congress certainly pressed its claim to speak on behalf of all Indians with tangible determination. Gandhi preached unity, but he had little of practical value to offer at that moment, and with matters now transcending the pulpit, Gandhi, in many respects, had become something of a liability.

On May 16, 1946, after initial dialogue with each side, the cabinet mission released its preliminary proposals for the composition of the new government. In these proposals, the creation of a separate Muslim Pakistan was ruled out, but at the same time, a wide enough crack was left in the door for a more general interpretation to be possible. What was proposed was a complicated federal system whereby a central government would be responsible for national affairs — foreign affairs, defense, transport, and communication — while a three-tier system of regional blocs would reserve wide powers for domestic administration. This would provide for independence as a British overseas dominion, fully engaged in the Commonwealth and remaining firmly within the British sphere of influence. It was a loosely configured concept that was all things to all people, and the prerequisite was simply that Indian politicians ratify it by accepting office as responsible ministers in the proposed government.

Jinnah and the Muslim league were quick to accept the plan, but Congress rejected it outright. Nehru held a press conference in Bombay declaring that Congress had agreed only to participate in the Constituent Assembly and regarded itself free to change or modify the Cabinet Mission Plan as it thought best. This prompted an immediate Muslim League walk out, which, no doubt, was the intention.

And so it went. Cripps might have felt that he had seen all of this before, and although British officials were formally required to discourage discussion of two states, it is unlikely that any of them saw any real alternative. This was confirmed at the end of July 1946 when Jinnah held a press conference at his Bombay home, where he declared once again his intention of creating Pakistan, intimating very generally that, if necessary, a violent struggle would be the means by which this would be achieved. When asked to specify, Jinnah responded with the comment, "Go to the Congress and ask them their plans. When they take you into their confidence I will take you into mine. Why do you expect me alone to sit with folded hands? I also am going to make trouble." The next day, he announced that August 16, 1946 would be "Direct Action Day". What this meant was left vague, but it was understood that meetings would be held here and there and no more than commonplace levels of disturbance encouraged simply to make a point. In general, this is what happened, but in one particular instance, in a sign of things to come, matters escalated beyond anything anyone could have foreseen.

The minutia of what led to the events in Calcutta on that day has been widely studied and debated, but what is clear is that communal violence on an unprecedented scale broke out. The general view of the matter is that violence was provoked first by Muslim demonstrators, but soon it became general, with a death toll estimated at between 7,000-10,000 Hindus, Muslims, and Sikhs. All sides considered their community the victims, and each blamed the other. The British authorities were charged with being slow to act, which is probably true. Preparations had certainly been inadequate, but no degree of preparation could really have prevented what took place. The violence continued for several days, sparking similar riots elsewhere, after which, for the next few months, clashes between the communities flared up periodically. In the aftermath, the British-brokered coalition government collapsed, and Jinnah announced an end to constitutional methods. "Today we have forged a pistol," he declared. "And [we] are in a position to use it."

Violence

"Any idea of a united India could never have worked and in my judgement would have led us to disaster." – Muhammad Ali Jinnah

August 1946 certainly was the turning point, and for the first time, elements within Congress itself began to air the possibility of a two-state solution. The British government retreated, recognizing that there was only so much that could be done and that ultimately the formula for independence lay in Indian hands. A deadline of no later than June 1948 was set for a transfer of power, which served clear notice on India to get its house in order. At more or less the same time, Prime Minister Attlee withdrew Lord Wavell as Governor General, replacing him with a more malleable personality in the form of Lord Louis Mountbatten, who was charged with overseeing the transition of power.

Mountbatten

Mountbatten, a fixture of the British aristocracy, was an odd, but perhaps inspired choice for this epoch-making appointment. Often criticized for his lack of intelligence, creativity, and leadership flair, he could well be regarded as a member of the very British class that thrived on Imperial India. He certainly enjoyed an august career and much imperial authority, based less on his ability than his birthright. To be appointed to this delicate diplomatic responsibility by a Labor prime minister was certainly unexpected, but perhaps the very Anglocentric nature of all three Indian nationalists in the picture, Gandhi included, demanded the involvement of such a British establishment figure. His instructions were simply to oversee the transition of power, get Britain out of India as cleanly and quickly as possible, and to avoid in the process any unnecessary damage to the reputation of Britain.

Matters were complicated a little by Mountbatten's personal friendship with Nehru, a fondness that was reciprocated by Nehru mainly in an untoward affection for Mountbatten's wife. Edwina Mountbatten, a powerful force in her own right, is rumored to have been intimate with Nehru and counted herself among the many European women who resided within the exclusive inner circle of the Mahatma. This comfortable union of the viceregal family and the Congress hierarchy had the effect of alienating Jinnah, who was always very chilly towards Mountbatten. Likewise, Mountbatten found the nervous, chain-smoking, and austere Jinnah a man entirely outside of his scope of understanding. His dealings with him, therefore, were stiff and reserved and without the easy familiarity that he enjoyed with Nehru and Gandhi.

In his first meeting with Jinnah on April 5, 1947, Mountbatten attended to the formality of persuading the Muslim leader to accept independence within a united India, but he was not in the least disturbed or surprised when this was rejected immediately. Thereafter, Mountbatten set to work preparing India for independence under the principle of partition. He brought forward the deadline six months, establishing August 15, 1947 as the provisional date of independence. This gave a total of four months for the complicated separation to be achieved. Congress by then had come to accept this inevitability, and only Gandhi, his power base now largely symbolic, continued to urge Mountbatten to persevere in searching for a formula for a united India. As an indication, some were apt to observe, of Gandhi's growing estrangement from reality, he urged Mountbatten to invite Jinnah to form a new central government, which Mountbatten wisely chose not to propose nor discuss with Gandhi's colleagues in the nationalist movement.

The first issue that Mountbatten was required to deal with was the question of the Princely States, and it is perhaps thanks to his own aristocratic origins that he was able to both sympathize with the erosion of hereditary rule but at the same time persuade the princes that their only course of action was to ally with one of the democratic nations in incubation. There were those kingdoms that would not, of course (namely Hyderabad, Jammu and Kashmir, and Junagadh), which sadly sowed the seeds of much future tension between India and Pakistan.

On June 3, 1947, Mountbatten presented his plan, refreshingly simple in the context of so much political complexity. The main points of the plans presented the likelihood of a sub-partition of Punjab and Bengal between the two states, but leaving the ultimate decision in the hands of the respective legislative assemblies of each province. The same was true for the northern provinces of Sind and Baluchistan, while a referendum would be held to determine the direction of the North West Frontier Province and the Sylhet district of Assam. No separate independence would be considered for the province of Bengal, and the future borders of the two states would be decided by a boundary commission.

Criticism was heaped on the plan from all sides for all kinds of reasons, but with the blunt determination of a sterile-minded man, Mountbatten simply closed the book on the matter and moved on to the next question. Congress accepted the proposals, recognizing perhaps, as the deadline approached, that the moment was not opportune for political bickering. Thereafter, all sides watched with interest as the work of the boundary commission began. The boundary commission was chaired by Sir Cyril John Radcliffe, 1st Viscount, a British lawyer, and Law Lord, supported by two Indian judges. The unenviable task handed to Radcliffe was to devise a territorial formula that would leave as many Hindus and Sikhs in India and as many Muslims in Pakistan as possible. For this purpose, broad delineations could be made of Hindu-dominated or Muslim-dominated regions, but no amount of creative penmanship could achieve a complete separation of the communities. The new boundaries were strategically announced only on August 14, 1947, the very day of Pakistan's independence and a day before India became independent. They were, therefore, a *fait accompli*, and in his typical style, Mountbatten let it be known that both sides could like it or leave it.

Meanwhile, in an atmosphere of almost frantic haste, the British Parliament began to debate the Indian Independence Act, which was granted royal assent on July 18, 1947. Provisions for a British withdrawal and the division of British India into two fully sovereign dominions of India and Pakistan were ratified before the boundaries of the new states had even been established.

As a result, some 14 million individuals, Muslim and Hindu, were stranded on the wrong side of their respective borders, and as the countdown to independence began, a mass migration of Hindus from Pakistan to India and of Muslims from India to Pakistan began. What followed was one of the greatest bouts of attempted genocide and ethnic cleansing in all of human history.

The partition is typically portrayed by history as an act of shameful abandonment by the British, but from the point of view of the British, who watched the horror play out as they were drawing up the gangplank, they were damned if they did and damned if they did not. The "Quit India" movement had announced both the Indian demand and the Indian haste to be rid of the British, but when the British did depart and the limitations imposed by their secular authority were lifted, India descended into anarchic violence and bloodshed. This prompted even greater criticism to be leveled against the British for leaving.

Be that as it may, however, Attlee, Wavell, and Mountbatten, and no doubt many others too realized that the time had come and that there would be no easy way to get the job done. If Mountbatten had been charged with achieving a difficult separation with a minimum of damage to the British reputation, then he probably failed, but at the same time, there was no real formula for success. Indians were ready to settle scores, and if British rule was all that was keeping them apart, then they were more than anxious to see the British gone.

Indeed, as the curtain began to fall on British India, Indians fell upon one another, and a thousand years of simmering antipathy exploded in an orgy of communal violence. The focus of violence in the immediate independence period tended to be concentrated in the Punjab and Bengal, the two Indian provinces that had themselves been partitioned by the delineation of boundaries. Both were regions relatively evenly populated by Hindus and Muslims, and the vast demographic shift that partition set in motion triggered a bout of retributional violence that favored none and spared none.

In the Punjab, some 4.5 million Hindus and Sikhs abandoned the western regions of the province and flooded into the east, while a higher number of Muslims migrated in the opposite direction. The British authorities, responsible for maintaining peace and order, were hopelessly overwhelmed by the scale of the violence, and in the end they mounted an inadequate and under-resourced response. By the time some order had been returned to the province (and even this was extremely limited), anywhere between 180,000 and 500,000 Hindus, Sikhs, and Muslims had perished, often under circumstances of excruciating violence.

The situation in Bengal, already partitioned in 1905, was somewhat less incendiary, but it too formed one of the numerous epicentres of violence. Several provincial cities were also rocked by communal violence, with Delhi, Bombay, Karachi, and Quetta in particular bearing the brunt. The violence was indiscriminate both in its perpetrators and victims. Peasants, the middle-classes, blue and white collar workers, religious persons, men and women, Hindus and Muslims were all implicated. Muslims who were forcibly removed from majority Hindu areas of India, their business and properties seized, made their way to Pakistan and subsequently joined the frenzy of anti-Hindu violence. Within the communities, fingers were pointed and continue to be pointed, but neither side can reasonably claim a monopoly on the role of victim or deflect culpability. It was communal violence in the true sense of the word.

During the initial independence phase, the figure typically quoted for general displacement is some 14 million, although many claim this is conservative and does not take into account those affected by the violence who did not migrate. The death toll also ranges widely, from 200,000-2 million. Truth be told, any figure within that range could plausibly be considered as good as any other.

The violence and mass refugee migrations continued into 1948, reaching a crescendo with the assassination of Gandhi on January 30 of that year. Throughout the violence, Gandhi had maintained his universalist position, appealing for calm and reconciliation and conducting regular inter-faith prayer vigils in various affected areas. On the day of his assassination, he was in Delhi, and as he was preparing for such a meeting, he was shot three times. His killer, Nathuram Godse, was a member of the extremist Hindu militant group Hindu Mahasabh, and the stated reason for his actions was Gandhi's accommodation of Muslims and advocacy of tolerance. Godse accused Gandhi of subjectivism and of acting as if only he had a monopoly of the truth. Godse, who had planned the assassination with, among others, fellow Hindu extremist Narayan Apte, was tried and convicted of murder. Both men were executed in 1949. The upswell of violence that followed Gandhi's death involved an inter-Hindu conflict as well as an increase in communal violence. Nathuram Godse was a Chitpavan Brahmin, and heavy reprisals were wrought against that community by various Congress supporters, most notably in the western Maharashtra State.

Godse

Further massacres were recorded across northern India and southern Pakistan, with, in addition to Punjab and Bengal, significant dislocation affecting the Sindh province. Sindh, now a province of Pakistan, hosted a large Hindu and Sikh minority, and it saw a mass exodus of some 800,000 Hindus to India, mainly to Bombay and Maharashtra. The death toll in this episode is unknown, but it was at least in the tens of thousands and possibly hundreds of thousands. More localized bouts of violence were recorded in Delhi, Alwar and Bharatpur, and Jammu and Kashmir.

Beginning in 1948, an orchestrated program gathered momentum on both sides of the border to begin the process of resettlement, and the dust of the whole brutal affair only began to settle toward the end of the decade.

Indian Independence Day is marked on August 15, and every year on that day, India rolls out a spectacle of pomp and ceremony that reflects in every detail the curious love affair the country still enjoys with Britain. The accoutrements of empire still decorate Indian military traditions, and the residues of British India remain visible almost everywhere. On that day in 1947, however, as Lord Mountbatten stood in his viceregal uniform, a figure from another era, and handed over power to the simply attired Indian leadership, a new age began.

As the British Raj slipped away into history and as the sun began to set on the British Empire, small nations across the world were watching very closely. Six years later, another venerable bastion of the British imperial age fell to a military coup. Egypt entered the revolutionary field, inspired by the emerging Cold War and strategically positioned astride the Suez Canal. The Suez Crisis, the British military intervention, and the British military humiliation finally alerted the British to a new reality. Soon the Gold Coast was independent, and then Nigeria, Jamaica, Kenya, Uganda, and many others were free as the dominos began to fall.

Many of those transitions were violent and many followed a similar pattern, but India remained the test case. The Indian and Pakistani individual relationship with Britain survived, but their relationship with one another was never healed. Partition is usually remembered for the sake of its violence, and violence certainly did occur on an epic scale. "Holocaust" is a word now frequently used, and each side still consistently blames the other. However, the violence was only a part of the picture. The Muslim-Hindu divide pre-existed all modern political machinations, and partition was an equalization simply waiting to happen. India and Pakistan are artificial creations of an imperial power that did not take any of this into account. As was true in many other cases and many other colonies, when the time came, the British were all too keen to jump ship, and the British were slow to accept responsibility for the aftermath or what could have been done differently.

One such result is the cold war between India and Pakistan that has been simmering since the partition. The frontier between India and Pakistan remains one of the most potentially volatile in the world, and these two societies, which have uneasily coexisted alongside one another for centuries, remain today as immiscible as oil and water.

Online Resources

Other British history titles by Charles River Editors

Other titles about the British Raj on Amazon

Bibliography

Barua, Pradeep P. *Gentlemen of the Raj: The Indian Army Officer Corps, 1817-1949*. Westport, CT: Praeger, 2003.

Carr, Robert. "Concession & Repression: British Rule in India 1857-1919: Robert Carr Assesses the Nature of British Rule in India during a Key, Transitional Phase," *History Review*, no. 52 (2005).

Cavendish, Richard. "The Black Hole of Calcutta." *History Today* Volume 56. Issue 6. June 2006.

Cross, Colin. *The Liberals in Power, 1905-1914.* London: Barrie and Rockliff, 1963.

Derbyshire, I. D. "Economic Change and the Railways in North India, 1860-1914." *Modern Asian Studies* 21, no. 3 (1987): 522.

Dewey, Clive. *Anglo-Indian Attitudes: Mind of the Indian Civil Service*. London: The Hambledon Press, 1993.

Francavilla, Domenico. "Interacting Legal Orders and Child Marriages in India." *American University Journal of Gender Social Policy and Law* 19, no. 2 (2011): 535-538.

Griffiths, Percival. *The British Impact on India*. London: MacDonald, 1952.

Guha, Ramachandra. "Churchill and Gandhi", *The Hindu Magazine*. June 19, 2005.

Kaushik, R.K. "The Men Who Ran the Raj." *Hindustan Times*. April 17, 2012.

Keay, John. *India: A History.* New York: Atlantic Monthly Press, 2000.

Kerr, Ian. *Engines of Change: The Railroads that Made India.* Westport, Connecticut: Praeger, 2007.

Kipling, Rudyard. *The Collected Poems of Rudyard Kipling*. Hertfordshire: Wordsworth Editions Limited, 2004.

Lalvani, Kartar. *The Making of India: The Untold Story of British Enterprise*. London: Bloomsbury Continuum, 2016.

Lewis, Martin Deming ed., *British in India: Imperialism or Trusteeship?* Boston: D.C. Heath, 1962.

Louis, William Roger, Porter, Andrew, and Alaine M. Low, eds., *The Oxford History of the British Empire,* vol. 3 (Oxford: Oxford University Press, 1999.

Macaulay, Thomas B. Bureau of Education. Selections from Educational Records, Part I (1781-1839). Edited by H. Sharp. Calcutta: Superintendent, Government Printing, 1920. Reprint. Delhi: National Archives of India, 1965, 107-117.

McLeod, John. *The History of India*. Westport, CT: Greenwood Press, 2002.

Macmillan, Margaret. *Women of the Raj: The Mothers, Wives, and Daughters of the British*

Empire in India. New York: Random House Trade Books, 2007.

Mahajan, Sneh. *British Foreign Policy, 1874-1914: The Role of India.* London: Routledge, 2002.

Masani, Zareer. *Indian Tales of the Raj.* Berkeley: University of California Press, 1987.

Misra, B. B. *The Indian Middle Classes: Their Growth in Modern Times.* London: Oxford University Press, 1961.

Planning Commission, Government of India, *The New India: Progress through Democracy.* New York: Macmillan, 1958.

Prasad, Ritika. *Tracks of Change: Railways and Everyday Life in Colonial India.* Daryaganj: Cambridge University Press, 2015.

Preston, John. "The British Were Imperialist Brutes? No, Britain Made India Great (says an Indian)". *UK Daily Mail*, 17 March 2016.

St. John, Ian. *The Making of the Raj: India under the East India Company.* Santa Barbara, CA: Praeger, 2012.

Sarkar, Tanika. "Women in South Asia: The Raj and After," *History Today*, September 1997.

Sunderland, Jabez T. *India in Bondage.* New York: Lewis Copeland Company, 1932.

Thompson, Edward. *Suttee: A Historical and Philosophical Enquiry into the Hindu Rite of Widow Burning.* London: George Allan and Unwin Ltd., 1928.

Von Albertini, Rudolf and Wirz, Albert. *European Colonial Rule, 1880-1940: The Impact of the West on India, Southeast Asia, and Africa*, trans. John G. Williamson. Westport, CT: Greenwood Press, 1982.

Walsh, Judith E. *Growing Up in British India: Indian Autobiographers on Childhood and Education under the Raj.* New York: Holmes & Meier, 1983.

Wolpert, Stanley. "A Mixed Legacy: From the Raj to Modern India," *Harvard International Review* 32, no. 4 (2011).

Wolpert, Stanley. *Gandhi's Passion: The Life and Legacy of Mahatma Gandhi.* New York: Oxford University Press, 2002.

Zachariah, Benjamin. *Nehru.* New York: Routledge, 2004.

Free Books by Charles River Editors

We have brand new titles available for free most days of the week. To see which of our titles are currently free, click on this link.

Discounted Books by Charles River Editors

We have titles at a discount price of just 99 cents everyday. To see which of our titles are currently 99 cents, click on this link.

Printed in Great Britain
by Amazon